A Life of

Prayer

By Cassondra Windwalker

Published by
Spiritbuilding Publishers
9700 Ferry Road, Waynesville, Ohio 45068

A LIFE OF PRAYER
By Cassondra Windwalker

ISBN: 978–0–9990684–5–8

Spiritbuilding

PUBLISHERS

spiritbuilding.com

Table of Contents

Dedicated to Dick Lambert,
beloved brother in Christ whose life typifies the fast
and to Faye Doughty, beloved sister in Christ
whose heart is a prayer realized.

CHAPTER ONE
⇒*What Is the Point?*⇐

WHY ARE YOU HERE?

Not why do you exist, but why are you here, in this moment, with this book in your hands? This first chapter isn't about answers, it's about questions. Why do we want to learn more about prayer?

For some of us, there's little to ask. Prayer is an occasional rote act, a tip of the hat to a divine power, a rabbit's-foot at bedtime, an acknowledgment of tradition at the dinner table. We rattle off comfortable phrases absorbed long ago from the mouths of others. In church services, it's a transitional trick to move us from one form of worship to another. At funerals, it's a means to offer comfort. At weddings, a come-to-order. We are often so familiar with certain turns of speech that we unconsciously open our eyes and lift our heads when someone veers too far from the rutted tracks we anticipate.

Others of us are quite at ease with spontaneous prayer. When we encounter disaster or grief or terrors, our first instinct is to stop, seize whatever hand is closest, and drop immediately into petition. Some people find this unexpectedly comforting and reassuring. Others are suspicious, taken aback, startled off-guard. They wonder if this is a show we are putting on, where our sense of decorum is, and hastily rattle off Jesus' admonition to pray in closets as a prop to their embarrassment.

Some of us live in a constant running monologue directed at God, an unspoken pattering of mostly thoughtless conversation picked up every few minutes throughout the day. We trust God implicitly with our parking spot dilemmas, the magical opening of a third cash register, our completely unnecessary drive on icy roads, and getting all green lights when we leave late for work. We take pride in our reliance on God for everyday living but have lost all sense of respect or awe in our approach, often muttering pleas while shimmying out of our clothes or standing in the shower or sitting on the toilet. We send up hasty intercessions between memes and GoFundMe notifications on our phones. And when we're faced with something legitimately, entirely, out of our hands, something that requires our complete and unqualified reliance on God, we are at a loss as to how to pray with deliberation. To drop to our knees, shut out the world for an hour or more, and pray aloud, with a single, unbroken intention is an impossibility.

I say we, because I have been all of these people, and I imagine many of you have been as well. Prayer can be a touchy subject, because aren't all Christians supposed to know exactly how to pray already? It's tempting to smile and nod when people say "rich prayer life" as if we know what in the world that is supposed to mean. No-one wants to step up and say, *I don't know how to do this, or I don't feel like anyone is listening, or why doesn't this work?* No-one wants to admit they feel awkward about prayer or have doubts about what it can accomplish. We all express gratitude when someone tells us they're praying for us, and then we wonder, but are you really? And what does that sound like? And why isn't it working?

Why isn't it working?

Perhaps this is the real reason you are reading this book. I imagine every believer has grappled with this question. When we come to God disconsolate and desperate, pouring out our hearts in urgent petition, and find ourselves refused, the grief and confusion is staggering. Did I not have enough faith? Am I doing this wrong? Does God not care? Is everything predetermined so that prayer has no practical effect at all anyway? Is God a being who demands constant acknowledgment and praise but has nothing to say in return?

These are hard questions. And while the chapters ahead will endeavor to answer these, there are some questions you must first answer for yourself.

Why do you want to understand prayer? Is your search outcome-focused or relationship-focused? What do you want to get from God that you hope prayer can supply?

It will also be important to examine what your prayer habits are now, before we move forward with this study. When do you pray, and how do you pray? What sort of prayers are most common for you—intercession for others, requests for self, praise, thanksgiving, repentance, or the laundry list prayer which clumps everything together at once. Or perhaps you rely on the hand-wave prayer: *to God who knows everything before we ask, please grant our petitions and forgive whatever transgressions we have committed.* I've often heard this one led even by elders and preachers at church gatherings. A prayer asking God to do incredible, unimaginably powerful things that we can't even be troubled to list, because, you know, the sermon is going to take too long already.

We call ourselves the family of God, but we're usually much closer to being the PTA or Homeowner's Association of God. We're in pretty close quarters and we share a common goal, but we always clear out the dirty laundry and put out the good china before inviting each other in. We struggle with transparency and weakness and doubts and flaws. We all want to look like we get it, we understand, we have it together. But true families know exactly who never makes their bed, who is scared of spiders, who eats Pop Tarts for dinner. And the beauty of God wanting to set us in families like a wounded sheep in the midst of a flock (Psalm 107:41) is that our family does know exactly what our weaknesses are. Knowing our weaknesses, they will strengthen us if they can and shield us if they cannot. This only works if we are willing to be honest and unfiltered and defenseless with each other.

So, if you're reading this book as part of a study group or Bible class, spend some time discussing these questions with each other. Talk about what your prayer life looks like now, what you think it accomplishes, what you want it to look like. What baffles or grieves you. What you're afraid of.

And if you're reading it alone, reach out to a fellow believer. A friend, a spouse, a coworker who bows her head with you at lunch. Tell them what you're reading and what you're wondering. Find out where they are in their journey. All these navigational points will help you find your own location on the path so you can make it safely through the woods.

Notes for Chapter 1

Chapter Two
⟹*Entrust to Truth*⟸

Augustine famously said in Confession Eleven of Book IV, "Entrust to Truth whatever you have from Truth, and you will lose nothing." Perhaps this is a poor but concise summary of God's litany of questions directed at Job at the close of that book. All that is real, all that is beautiful, and all that is good, proceeds from truth.

In Job chapters 38—41, God calls on Job to gather himself and answer. This exchange is noteworthy for many reasons. Few instances are given of God engaging in literal dialogue with people. Here, God speaks directly and personally to Job. He completely disregards the foolish friends who had condemned Job as the cause of his own downfall (and Elihu) aside from telling Job that they speak from ignorance and implying that he does not know them.

God's arrival on the scene corrects the misapprehensions of both Job and his friends and signals the restoration of Job's prosperity, health, and joy, but he does not comfort Job with soft speech or reassurances. He never explains to Job the catalyst of his misfortunes. He does not justify his own apparent absence. Yet from Job's response in 42:1–6, it is clear that Job is comforted and reassured.

What are we missing? For many of us, the book of Job is itself a challenge of faith. Knowing the drama that unfolded in the heavenly court prior to Job's suffering makes it almost more troubling, not less so, that God permitted this devastation to unfold. And God's eventual conversation with Job may feel cold, unfeeling, even hostile, as God unfurls all his power and mystery and glory in the face of Job's helplessness and agony. It's uncomfortable to admit this. What sort of God can look at a man whose children are dead, who is literally in the dirt in poverty and sickness, and speak of oceans and stars and eagles and fish?

Truth can speak this way. And Job, who had entrusted all that he loved to Truth, heard it and was comforted.

In the first chapter of the book, we learn that Job offered his children up to God in prayer and sacrifice continually. We know from God's description of Job that his trust and reliance in God in all things was complete. When Job realizes his entire life has been stolen away from him, his children and his servants dead, his livelihood destroyed, he states his willingness to return to God as he came into the world—utterly naked.

What to our ears, to our hearts that are perhaps weaker in faith than Job, sounds like a brutally chilling indictment of man's ignorance before God, actually was reassurance to Job. Every question God asks, Job knows the answer. The answer is God. The answer is Truth. The God to whom Job has entrusted his children and his life and his soul was every bit as powerful and creative and beautiful and unknowable as Job had believed. His faith had not been misplaced. Everything real that Job had given over to that God was still safe. Although the corporeal reality around Job seemed to prove the uselessness of his prayers, God was promising him that he was more than mighty enough to keep what Job had committed into his hands.

Are our prayers powerless? Perhaps we are praying to a powerless God, one we have unwittingly plastered together ourselves out of wishes and hopes and misconceptions, self-righteousness and justification, wood and stone. It is easy to build a God we can define, whose laws and motivations we can list in neat bullet points. But this sort of God requires a lot of direction. So we pray to him with painful exactitude.

Dear Father, Please help me get this new job, but I need the night shift so I can get the kids to school, and let them wait to call me till I've had a chance to take my vacation time.

Dear Father, Please heal my sister from her cancer before she finds out her husband is cheating on her because I only have one spare bedroom and she has three kids.

Dear Father, Please bring rain to put out the wildfire but don't let the rivers flood.

Dear Father, Please help the good people [people I love] and defeat the bad people [people I don't love] and don't ask me to sacrifice too much to make that happen.

We worry God might not really understand all the possible outcomes of his rash actions on our behalf, so we try to fence our requests as precisely as possible along the property lines we are willing to own. Other times our trouble is the opposite: we worry that Paul wasn't exaggerating at all when he wrote to the Ephesians that God is "able to do exceeding abundantly above all we ask or think" (3:20). We are more comfortable with a leashed deity, one whose intentions we can anticipate and whose power will be delicately applied only as much as we wish and no more. We may not want a fierce and wild and unpredictable Being expending his will and power on our behalf.

As a meditation technique, then, prayer may be useful enough in helping us identify who we are and what we want, but until we are willing to trust Truth with ourselves and all that we love, our voices will never do more than echo back at us from the walls of our own houses. We must be willing to believe in Him whom we cannot know, we must trust what we cannot comprehend, we must surrender without caveat everything we would hold most tightly.

Are there people or things or ideas in our lives that we love too little to give to God? It doesn't feel that way. It feels like we love them too much. We are afraid to let them get out of our reach. Afraid to watch them disappear down a path that isn't yet ours to follow, that may never be. But it's like the mother caught in the burning building with her child in her arms. All her instinct screams at her to hold fast, to never let that child go. But the only way to save the child is to let them go, to trust that the arms of the firefighter are strong enough and big enough to carry the child to safety.

We must make careful inventory of our treasures and then relinquish them entirely. All that we cling to becomes ash in the end.

CHAPTER THREE
⇒*Teach Me Thy Ways*⇐

OFTEN WE APPROACH GOD with the intention of bending him to our will. This isn't something we acknowledge, of course, or perhaps even recognize in ourselves, but a cursory examination of our requests soon makes this plain. To pray, to fast, is not to send a letter or shoot off an e-mail or instant message to the divine. To pray is to step into the court of God, to dwell with him in a space marked as our own by the blood of his Son. It is a communion of our soul with his.

Faith is the door through which we enter this place. We come into his presence not to make demands but to listen to his voice, to dwell in his love, to bring into ourselves the consummation of his will.

People recount the tale of the thief on the cross for many reasons, but seldom do we consider the request he made of Christ. "Lord, remember me when thou comest into thy kingdom" (Luke 23:42). After hours of unspeakable anguish, the thief has clearly recognized the divine nature of his fellow sufferer, the totality of his power. What is amazing is what he does not ask. He does not ask Jesus to spare his life. He does not ask Jesus to end his suffering. He asks Jesus to remember him. Somehow, in what ought to have been a moment of abject despair, the thief enters the presence of God and apprehends his will. For this, Jesus assures him of their unbroken walk together—not just that the thief would enter paradise, but that he would be there with Jesus himself.

In her book *Holy the Firm,* Annie Dillard says, "Teach me Thy ways, O Lord, is like all prayers a rash one, and one I cannot but recommend." True prayer is indeed a dangerous, reckless act subversive to the powers that be in this world. To enter into a dialogue with the Creator, to submit our own intentions entirely to his, transforms not only ourselves but necessarily the world itself. We cannot serve God without serving our fellow man, and we cannot serve our fellow man without revolutionizing our society.

The passage to which Annie Dillard refers is Psalm 86. The psalmist recounts the mercy and love and longsuffering of God, his grace and truth and power, his outstretched arm, and relays his desire to walk that same path. *Unite my heart,* he pleads. What a beautiful concept, for our hearts to be whole and undivided in their devotion to the divine nature.

When we, like the thief, are consumed by physical pain or absolute heartbreak, do we ask God to remove our agony? Or do we ask him to remember us, to carry us with him?

It is not wrong to ask God to deliver us from our troubles. The scriptures are full of examples of these requests and in many cases, of God's subsequent salvation. Jesus himself not only instructs us to ask our Father for all we require but welcomes us to ask him again and again. James, Jesus' earthly brother, urges us in 1:6 to ask in faith, doubting nothing. Our God is not heedless of our petitions: to the contrary, he can and will answer us with power.

Faith, however, is no small thing. We must not only have faith that he will answer us, we must have faith in who he is. Knowing him for who he is and not who we want him to be, we must comprehend all that is terrifying and all-consuming and other and still approach him fearlessly, made perfect in love. We must ask for everything we need and desire at the same moment we surrender every longing to his will. We must remake our own selfishnesses into servanthood.

"God is love; and he that dwelleth in love dwelleth in God, and God in him. Herein is our love made perfect, that we may have boldness in the day of judgment: because as he is, so are we in this world. There is no fear in love; but perfect love casteth out fear, because fear hath torment. He that feareth is not made perfect in love" (I John 4:16–18).

What survives the flame but fire itself? If we are to stand in God's presence and not be destroyed, we must partake of that same searing glory. By accepting God's nature fully into our own and allowing it to transform us, we are able to walk into the blaze without fear, complete in love.

Christianity is a devotion of mysteries. Jesus told his disciples that the only way to truly be children of the Father was to "love your enemies, bless them that curse you, do good to them that hate you, pray for them that despitefully use you and persecute you" (Matthew 5:44–45). The admonition to prayer is not one of lip-service. Here Jesus acknowledges the transformative nature of the sincere prayer. It is not possible to pray for our enemies without being ourselves changed, altered, glorified. Prayer is not the empty, rote mouthing of appropriate words and phrases: it is powerful and metamorphic and immediate.

To live in faith, then, is to live in love.

The more interior and sacrificial our conversations with God, the more devoted we will become to serving those around us. It is impossible to ask God to deliver others from suffering unless we are willing to be the instrument he uses for that deliverance. When we are fully spent in our love for others, we are fearlessly able to commit into God's hands all that we are unable to accomplish and be absolutely assured of his work on our behalf. We can ask for the miraculous, nothing doubting, because of the miracle he has accomplished in us already: the unbroken union of our imperfect selves with his perfect will.

So here we stand, staring at the door of faith which will open to us the chamber of our God, our Father, our Brother, our Paraclete. Within that room is all love, all hope, all power. But we must shed our secret selves before we enter. All the pieces of ourselves that we keep back from God, our willful desires, our hatreds, our prejudices, the meanness we allow ourselves, the justifications and excuses, must die here before we walk through.

Which of God's ways are we still afraid to learn? What sacrifice do we fear to make, what price is too high? Which of our enemies do we still beg leave to hate?

Notes for Chapter 3

Notes for Chapter 3

Chapter Four
≋ *The Mutable God* ≋

The title of this chapter likely has you squirming a bit in your seat. Isn't God immutable? Unchanging? Not according to the Bible. His nature—that of love and truth—is unchanging. His word is steadfast. It is impossible for him to lie. All these things are true. But if you really believe God is unchanging, then why do you pray at all, aside from prayers of praise and thanksgiving?

Of all the chapters in the book, this may be the most uncomfortable, the most challenging. Many of us have heard, and many of us have said things such as *everything that happens is under God's control or God has a plan for you.* In some ways, these statements are true. God created this world, its natural systems and laws. But by granting us free will, along with all the consequences of that, he relinquished his control over our actions. He may or may not choose to intervene in the natural world, but he will not alter our decisions.

God's plan for us is that we will love him and our fellow man, that we will accept salvation and share it with others, but he is not going to dictate how and where we do that. Anywhere, absolutely anywhere, we can accomplish this plan he has set for us. There is no place and no point in time we cannot do this. If our choices or our circumstances have brought us to Guatemala, to prison, to a nursing home, to a Coast Guard ship, to a park bench, or to a palace, God's plan for us is the same. All he asks of us is to do the good we are able, where we are. He doesn't care if we're a garbage collector or a doctor or a preacher or a disc jockey. He cares what we do in the space where we find ourselves.

In some ways this might be frightening, because if there is no single right destiny for our lives, then we'll never be able to rest in complacency, certain we have landed where we belong. On the other hand, we can be assured that wherever our course is leading, we are useful to God where we are.

The other vital aspect to this understanding is that God is never responsible for the evil in this world. It is never God's will or part of his plan for children to be murdered, for people to be raped, for cruelty and selfishness and greed to triumph in this world. These things happen in spite of God's plan, because free will dictates they must be permitted. God grieves even more than we do when wickedness reigns. He does not smile and nod and congratulate himself on a masterful plan. He mourns our choices: he is not chargeable for them. It provides no comfort when believers offer solace to the suffering by assuring them that God is liable for the evil that has entered their lives.

However, while God allows us the freedom and consequences of our choices, he is still vitally engaged in our daily lives. He is not a God unmoved by our plights and our victories. He is a relational God who not only asks us to walk with him, but who himself walked among us so that he might understand our sufferings and our temptations as a purely spiritual being never could. He invites us to come to him with our longings and desires and fears so that we might be strengthened and fed and consoled.

While God might change his mind on our behalf, his lovingkindness, as expressed by the Hebrew word *chesed,* never alters. Psalm 136 states that his lovingkindness endures forever. This word is found 249 times in the Old Testament. It is much more than simple love or affection. Also sometimes translated steadfast love or mercy, *chesed* can be defined as unfailing devotion in the context of a covenant relationship. More than a feeling, it is a promise that is always kept, a yearning that places the higher good of the recipient as the greatest consummation of the lover's intent.

This God, who aches for us, does not desire only the echo of his own existence lauded at him in our prayers. The book of Hebrews speaks beautifully to the deeply intimate relationship Jesus sacrificed all that he was so that he might build with us. He is "not a high priest who cannot be touched with the feeling of our infirmities, but was in all points tempted like as we are, yet without sin. Let us therefore come boldly unto the throne of grace, that we may obtain mercy, and find grace to help in time of need" (Hebrews 4:15–16). Jesus experienced all that it means to be human and mortal in order to be a servant on our behalf, but his labors for us did not end with his death and resurrection.

"This Jesus, because he continueth forever, hath an unchangeable priesthood. Wherefore he is also able to save them to the uttermost that come unto God by him, seeing he ever liveth to make intercession for them" (Hebrews 7:24–25). Even today, he continues to stand between us and our Father, the mediator of our hearts. And he does not work alone for us: the Holy Spirit translates our abject pleadings for us as well. "The Spirit also helpeth our infirmities: for we know not what we should pray for as we ought: but the Spirit himself maketh intercession for us with groanings that cannot be uttered. And he that searcheth the hearts [Jesus] knoweth what is the mind of the Spirit, because he maketh intercession for the saints according to the will of God" (Romans 8:26–27).

If our prayers were nothing more than incense offered up as praise and thanksgiving to our God, there would be no need for translation and intercession on our behalf. Our Brother and the Comforter work together to relay our yearnings to God, even when we ourselves don't know what to ask or how to speak.

And God has chosen to show himself to us as a God who can be persuaded, who can be touched for our sakes. He is willing, eager, to engage with us. As a being devoid of dishonesty in any form, he never pretends to entertain our desires. He is not disingenuous in his speech with us. What he says is true and pure and transparent.

In Exodus 32:9–14, God tells the story of the time he was determined to completely destroy the children of Israel and make a nation entirely of Moses' line, which would have still allowed him to keep his promise to Abraham. Moses pleads with God, and God says that he changed his mind—he "repented" because of Moses' words. Man does not make this claim—God makes it of himself. He chooses to portray himself as a being who can be affected by our words. In Luke 11:9–13, Jesus explicitly states that we will be given that for which we ask. This necessarily implies that if we do not ask, we will not be given. God will change his mind, choose his course, based on our address to him. We must ask, we must seek, we must knock.

In the examples Jesus lists in the preceding verses, those of the sympathetic friend and the loving father, he makes it plain that God's response to us is an emotional response. It is the response of love to longing.

Jeremiah 18 describes a God who is not only capable of changing his mind about people and nations, but willing to do suddenly, deftly. Just as God may swiftly bring judgment on the cruel, so he may amend and offer mercy to the penitent. His nature is unaltered, but his will, his decisions are absolutely affected by our choices and our prayers to him.

This relationship we have with our Creator, however, is complex and many-faceted. He is not an online shopping list or a bank account into which we deposit and withdraw at will. When we humbly approach him in prayer, when we starve our flesh so that our souls may enter his presence with the clarity of a fast, we do so in the context of the connection we share, a connection knotted fast by the bloody hands of his own Son.

The proper prayer and the strictest fast do not purchase our requests. Prayers and fasts are the function of our souls' yearning toward God, the quiet and steadfast communion we share with his will and his love and his truth. To even enter his presence, we must first acknowledge our own understanding is meager and broken. What we ask may not be our own good. Or perhaps it is a good to us but an unbearable suffering to someone whose existence we do not even perceive. God will never deny us any good. But we must be wary not to imagine that our comprehension of the world is sufficient to flawlessly know what is good.

There is more good and more real than our poor senses apprehend. And there is more powerful evil at work than we know. If we are not able to submit our longings to the will of God, then we neither believe in his power nor in his goodness. If we know that he is both good and mighty, then we can rest at peace, knowing that he fully hears the cries of our hearts and that he always gives us everything that is our good and the good of the world. What he denies is only what would bring more suffering, whether we can see that or not.

So who is your God? Has he removed himself from the world of men and hears none of their petitions? Does he hear you and not care? Does he care but is powerless to help? Or is he the Father of *chesed,* of steadfast, unfailing devotion, who hears, who is moved, who is powerful, who gives only good gifts to his children?

_____
_____
_____
_____
_____
_____
_____
_____
_____
_____
_____
_____
_____
_____
_____
_____
_____
_____
_____
_____
_____
_____
_____
_____
_____
_____
_____
_____

Chapter Five
═How to Pray═

SOMETIMES WE BRISTLE AT the concept that there is a way to pray. The idea we do not simply instinctively know how to address our Creator, or that there could be a right and a wrong means of approaching him, puts up our hackles. Didn't Jesus break down the wall of separation between God and humankind with his sacrifice? Doesn't our Father invite all people, everywhere, to come to him as they are and be cleansed, regardless of ritual or rote repetitions?

Probably part of the disconnect arrives from the fact that we likely would instinctively understand, as poor clay-bound creatures, how to address our Creator, but we have long since renamed ourselves conquerors and dressed God down into a being neatly contained in church buildings and leather-bound pages. Both the humility and the mercy requisite to a conversation with the Creator of universes are lacking in many of us. So instruction is necessary. The deer and the whale, the hawk and the chameleon, need no schooling to speak to God, but mankind is another matter.

The Bible contains many powerful and effective prayers offered to God: Hannah's abject pleading, David's earnest transparency, Hagar's startled submission, Mary's triumphant praise, Daniel's continual devotion. While we will examine the various types of prayer in the coming chapters, here we are concerned simply with *how* we pray, any prayer we offer. For this study, we will look at Jesus' model prayer for his disciples in Luke 11:1–13 and his own personal prayer to the Father in John 17.

The model prayer is fascinating precisely because it is that: a skeleton designed entirely for us, the petitioners, to hang our pitiful skins upon. Jesus provides this outline because his disciples asked him to. As such, its instruction is invaluable. Unfortunately, many people have adopted it in just the spirit that Jesus most decried: an automatic laundry list recitation, a memory verse compelled to service in times of panic, a magical charm to ward off evil. If we understand he is teaching his disciples *how* to pray, and not what to pray, we will glean much more from these brief passages.

The beauty of prayer lies in its radical dissimilarity with a phone call, a letter, an email, or a text. There is nothing long-distance about prayer. Prayer is immediate and intimate. When we pray, we do not cast our words across an immeasurable heaven, hoping some particle of our intention will land at our King's feet. When we pray, we enter the court of our Father, our Brother, and the Spirit. Prayer dwells in the presence of God. Prayer brings us, in all our defect, with all our failings and yearnings, into the real and literal love of God.

So while our prayer may be constant, it cannot be casual. The first thing Jesus teaches his disciples in Luke is to build that space in their hearts where they acknowledge God for who he is and breathe in his being. *Hallowed be thy name, thy kingdom come, thy will be done, as in heaven, so on earth.* It is impossible to know our Father as he is and not be awed, humbled, comforted, warmed. This is not the god of the Amazon shopping cart or charm bracelet. This is the sustainer of the universe and the weaver of our existence.

Jesus reassures his disciples that they are to come to God with even the most carnal and basic of needs. In the same breath that he claims God as the ruler of heaven, he reminds us he is deeply engaged in our ordinary, everyday life. There is no task too great for God, but there is also no task too small. The God who mourns the sparrows as they fall, who is heart-stricken by the widow who gives her last coin, who measures men's faith by mustard seeds, cares for our small sorrows and small joys as no other god could. We rely on God for our spiritual strength; we must likewise rely on him utterly, fearlessly, trustingly for our physical strength. He will supply all we require to triumph over evil and live in peace with him.

We can recite demands and recount fears all we like, but as it impossible for us to approach God without humility, it is impossible to approach him without mercy. We can only enter the court of God naked and without defense. We cannot hide or disguise any of our flaws. And we cannot ask him to look on our deformities and name us beautiful and beloved if we withhold that same grace from others. Forgiveness, compassion, kindness are prerequisites to prayer.

Jesus' prayer in John 17 is nothing like the model prayer in its verbiage. Heart-wrenching, pitiful, and unspeakably noble by turns, this final conversation between Father and Son before the cross nonetheless mirrors the model prayer in its spirit. The absolute sovereignty of the Father and the complete trust of the Son in him frames every word. Jesus places all his hope only in the Father, offers up all he has achieved and asks God to perfectly accomplish the rest. He pleads for those whom he loves and for those yet to come. He takes his solace and comfort in the relationship he has with the Father, the knowledge that this love is eternal and supernal to all suffering.

The contemplative Thomas Merton made the point that "we do not pray for the sake of praying, but for the sake of being heard (*Thoughts in Solitude.*)" Our prayers mean nothing unless we bide in the absolute confidence that God not only hears but answers. At this moment in Jesus's existence on earth, he has never been in greater need than this moment. Never has he been under more pressure or experienced more terror, more dread. He did not pray because it was his duty: he prayed because he desperately, earnestly craved the consolation only prayer offers. If he was going to face what lay ahead, he needed his Father's presence.

"The effectual fervent prayer of a righteous man availeth much" (James 5:16), but prayer is also an end to itself. Through prayer we obtain the benevolence and providence of God, we are forgiven of our trespasses, we grow in wisdom and mercy and grace. We should not forget, though, the incredible gift of simply being in the presence of God. The time we spend speaking with him, meditating on his word and his will with our whole soul and body, is precious and powerful in its own right.

Modern western society often discounts the value of fasting in prayer, if they even recognize it at all as anything outside of a diet fad or an outdated cultural norm from any culture but their own. In Matthew 9:14–15, Jesus states that his disciples will fast when he is no longer with them. Presence, then, is a signal aspect of the fast. By removing all of our will and purpose from supplying the needs of the flesh, we draw nearer to the pure spirit of God. The discipline and deliberation required of a fast allow us to pray with greater intensity and focus. We distill all our being, for the duration of the fast, into a continual walk with God. We dedicate those hours to remaining in his presence.

The mechanics of a fast are not dictated anywhere in the Bible. Some people have medical conditions that would make a complete fast dangerous rather than edifying. Sometimes those people are able to simply limit themselves to a certain number of calories, eating only particular foods, and consider that their fast. A penitent may fast for a day or three days or a week. Sometimes people fast out of desperate need: cancer or homelessness is knocking at their door, a beloved is addicted to drugs, their heart is broken. Other times people may fast as part of their personal relationship with God, where they choose to dedicate the first of every month or a day of every week to communion with God. Fasting is a prayer of the body, a yearning of the entire being toward the Creator. Like the spoken prayer, its times and durations are not prescribed.

As we look forward to the various types of prayers outlined in the coming chapters, we should examine our practices as they are now. Are there any techniques you personally have used to help you enter wholly into the presence of God? Are there types of language or affects that make prayer more or less intimate for you? Phrases that are comforting and meaningful to one person may have a completely different impact on someone else. Whether you pray kneeling, reclining, or hands raised is beside the point, as long as your position is representative of your reverence and your intimacy with God. Once our prayer becomes representative of our traditions rather than our hearts, then it falls dead to the ground.

Have you ever fasted? Why or why not? How often are your prayers the consequence of habit rather than a deliberate dialogue with the Creator? Do you pray merely to speak, or do you wait and listen for the answers as well?

Notes for Chapter 5

CHAPTER SIX

⇒*Prayers of Thanksgiving*⇐

THE NEXT FOUR CHAPTERS explore specific types of prayers as independent concepts. Perhaps the most common type of prayer is the bullet-point prayer. These take many forms, but often look something like a hastily-muttered generic thanks followed by the meat of the supplication—all the things we want. If we remember, we may tack on a request for forgiveness of any sins we may have committed.

I encourage you to set some time aside as you read through these chapters for deliberate, intentional, focused prayers. A space we enter into with God, a space entirely for gratitude and humility and submission, imbues the penitent with peace that can be found nowhere else. Setting aside every fear, every longing, every doubt, every desire for the sake of thanks powerfully reshapes our soul into a being more like the Spirit, a being of "love, joy, peace, longsuffering, kindness, goodness, faithfulness, meekness and temperance (Galatians 5:22–23.)" To walk in the Spirit is fundamentally to walk in a state of deep and abiding gratitude.

A prayer of thanksgiving assumes our complete reliance on God. It is an acknowledgment that He alone is the origin of all that is good, beautiful, and real. Thanksgiving is obeisance, a genuflection of the self toward the Truth that is selfless. Thanksgiving necessarily tends toward mercy, because in admitting our own helplessness, we must denounce any imagined superiority over those around us. The one who has been given much, must give much again. Those who hoard their blessings lack genuine gratitude and so are incapable of kindness.

One of the most beautiful aspects of Christianity is its absence of circumscription. A person of any developmental ability, speaking in any language, using the constructs of any culture, can offer prayer up to God and find themselves fully submerged in His presence. Our Father grants universal grace, unaffected by the paltry and temporary differences we imagine define us. The Bible offers many varied examples: Miriam's grateful song, David's triumphant dance, Paul's continual and earnest poetry, but does not limit our expression to these. Our reverence and our open, broken hearts are the only relics required.

With Jesus as our high priest (Hebrews 3:1), we are urged to "offer the sacrifice of praise to God continually, that is, the fruit of our lips giving thanks to his name" (Hebrews 13:17). Thanksgiving is our resting state, and we find ourselves continually and spontaneously expressing this. In 4:16 of the same book, the writer urges us to "come boldly to the throne of grace." Prayer, our communion with the Creator, is not something to be hesitantly and occasionally approached with fearful feet. It is a condition of our existence. This is how Paul was able to instruct the Christians at Thessalonica to "pray without ceasing." Our friendship with God is as ubiquitous as breathing.

God cannot lie, and he does not expect us to come to him draped in the falsehood of mock happiness masquerading as piety. Sometimes our lives are absolutely wrecked with tragedy and trial. The Psalms are an excellent resource for examples of completely transparent reliance on God. The writer is angry, despairing, giddy, gracious, and at peace by turns. He comes to God as he is and offers all of that and only that at God's feet. Even our prayers of thanksgiving need not be oblivious to grief. In II Samuel 12, when David's infant son dies, his worship to God is not out of gratitude that he lost his son, but that he would one day be reunited with him. False or forced thanksgiving is not welcome before God and merits our souls nothing.

However, the more difficult the hour, the more powerful the act of giving thanks. It may be that literally every circumstance in our own lives provokes only dread, fear, and pain. To find what is beautiful and precious still we must look far afield. So we become a creature whose vision more nearly approaches that of the Creator, able to see outside of our own narrow experience and into the wonders of the universal life of which we partake. This understanding may not ease our suffering, but it offers a glittering thread of hope to which we may cling in our present darkness.

Many examples of grateful prayer are found in the Bible. Three psalms of thanksgiving that fully acknowledge the ugliness of life while still wholly offering up gratitude are Psalms 18, 30, and 34. Prayers of thanksgiving always embody hope as well. Recognizing the love of God and his steadfast mercy toward his us, his unfailing labors on our behalf, reminds us that he is at work in even the blackest hours.

"Faith is the assurance of things hoped for, a conviction of things not seen" (Hebrews 11:1). We do not rely on faith for our thanksgiving. Our world is full of actual, present riches, beauties, and glories perpetually restored on our behalf. All created things consist in Christ (Colossians 1:16–17.) Moreover, the persistence of goodness, of kindness, in the abundance of so much selfishness and cruelty stands witness to the sustaining blessings of the Lord. All that is good proceeds from him and lives in him. Our sincere thanks contributes to and partakes in this body of beauty.

Often the only time we approach God is when we need something. It's not deliberate on our part: we just don't think about him till we need him. Spontaneous prayers of petition are far more common than spontaneous prayers of thanksgiving. Like it or not, this is a natural outgrowth of our innate selfishness. We're quick to recognize when we need something, less quick to recognize when we've been given something. Cultivating an attitude of thanksgiving requires intent on our part. It's who we choose to be.

Commit yourself to at least one prayer of thanksgiving a day. A prayer when you don't ask for anything, don't bring a litany of woes and worries, but only stand a moment with God and tell him that yes, you have seen his gifts. You have opened them and been blessed by them. Tell him how poor you would be without him and how incredibly rich you are with him.

These prayers may last a minute or ten or an hour. I suspect they will get longer the more often you attempt them. When we begin listing the providences of God, we are soon overwhelmed with the impossibility of truly recounting them. Regardless of the length of your prayers or the eloquence of your words, the grace you will carry through the rest of your day will be immeasurable. I think you will find yourself yearning to return to that place, that you will come to crave the solace and peace of sitting at your Father's knee with your Brother's hand on your head, naming aloud what is true, what is honorable, what is just, what is pure, what is lovely, what is reputable, what is virtuous, what is praiseworthy (Philippians 4:8).

If you are reading this book along with other believers, consider writing down a prayer of thanksgiving to share with others. Sometimes we are so self-conscious, even before our Maker, judging as inadequate our attempts to reach him. Our Father hears our hearts, our Brother sympathizes with our agonies, our Comforter relays our confusion and our unutterable griefs. Listening to one another as we approach God, hearing all the unique and particular and personal and intimate variants of our language and our thoughts, can encourage, edify, and embolden us in our entrance to our Father's court.

Notes for Chapter 6

Notes for Chapter 6

CHAPTER SEVEN
⟹*Prayers of Intercession*⟸

IN SOME WAYS this chapter is the crux of the book. Intercessory prayer, whether the intervention we seek is for our own part or on behalf of others, requires the greatest faith. Ironically, it is the most likely prayer to be uttered by the unbeliever. When people have no other hope, they will often call on a god in whom they do not even believe with the same surety a person buys a lottery ticket. But sometimes the pleadings of so-called believers signal no greater assurance.

Even when Jesus walked the earth and performed miracles in the presence of huge crowds, he was astounded by the faith of the centurion who asked him to heal his servant because his absolute certainty in Jesus' ability was so singular. Jesus' closest disciples were not so sure of his power as this man was. We may find ourselves similarly disposed. It's hardly unusual for most of us to pray after we have done all we can do ourselves, rather than before we begin. When we do finally bring our requests to God, we often hedge our bets, temper our expectations, with carefully constructed speech: we don't ask him to heal, we ask him to "be with the doctors." We don't ask him to save, we ask him to comfort. We don't ask him to provide, only to sustain.

Intercessory prayer, like every intersection of our faith with the being of God, rests on a paradox. The only deity with the power to help us necessarily sees and knows and comprehends all that we do not. Any request we bring to him we must simultaneously surrender with perfect faith that he is the gift-giver, gracious father, devoted brother, and still stand willing to accept him withholding the very thing we want most. We must believe he waits, ready to give us every good thing we ask, and that he may keep from us those very things, without telling us why.

A flawless example of this double-mindedness of the faithful is given in Daniel 3:13–27. Shadrach, Meshach, and Abednego have been sentenced to death in a fiery furnace for refusing to worship the idols of Babylon. King Nebuchadnezzar offers them one last chance to save themselves, and they give this stirring reply, "We are not careful to answer thee in this matter. If it be so, our God whom we serve is able to deliver us from the burning fiery furnace, and he will deliver us out of thine hand, o king. But if not, be it known unto thee, o king, that we will not serve thy gods, nor worship the golden image which thou hast set up."

These men had no doubt their God could and would save them, but they were equally at peace with the knowledge he might decide not to. Their faith did not rely on God's willingness to see the world as they saw it or give them what they wanted, even at the cost of their own lives. And certainly, while God did save them from this fate, eventually they did die. Our faith is not intended to deliver us from trials but bridge us through them.

But can God be persuaded from his course? The Bible tells us and shows us, indubitably, that he can. Existing as he does entirely in the spirit, he does not regard the things of the flesh as we do, but he is willing to be swayed nonetheless. He is not a dictator but a parent. He wants a relationship with us, and to this end, he invites us to influence him through our dialogue with him. Like many of the concepts in this book, this may feel uncomfortable for us to acknowledge. But the scriptures are clear on this point.

Samson calls on God for one last act of vengeance. Hezekiah begs for more years. Hannah asks for a son. Job intercedes on behalf of his friends. Moses prays for the fire of God to be quenched. Elisha pleads with God to raise the widow's son, and later, to reveal the host of his angelic army to one who doubted. To each of these requests, God responds with power and affirmation.

God does not only ask us to infer his willingness to be entreated. He tells us to pray to him on behalf of ourselves, on behalf of those we love, on behalf of our enemies. In Philippians 4:6, we are told to bring every request to God and to worry for nothing. In I Timothy 2:1, Paul says that above all things, we are to pray on behalf of others. In I John 5:16, the apostle tells us that when we pray for a brother in sin, God will grant life. Throughout the epistles to the various churches, Paul prays for the wisdom, strength, sanctification, and survival of the faithful, and begs them to pray for him as well. In II Timothy 4:16, Paul echoes the sentiments of Stephen and Jesus when he asks God to forgive others for the wrongs they have committed against him. Jesus himself instructed us to pray for those who persecute us.

Prayer on behalf of others is more than a mercy; it is a requirement. In I Samuel 12:23, Samuel states that he would be committing a sin against the Lord if he failed to pray for the people of Israel. Jesus tells us in Matthew 6:21 that our hearts and our treasures are never divided. Prayer is the chamber that holds both. We cannot claim we love our fellow man if we do not pray for him. Henry Nouwen wrote in *Discernment* that prayers of intercession create an inner community of the heart.

It is impossible to pray for anyone, even a stranger, over a period of time and not become invested in their wellbeing. We cannot pray to God for someone's good and then do them evil. Intercessory prayer does not only bring God into the room, it brings us fully into the room as well. When we call on God, he calls on us to be nearer to the divine for which we long. And while the catchphrase of "thoughts and prayers" is often decried, Paul refers to the prayers of the fellowship as being substantively helpful, not just emotionally gratifying, in II Corinthians 1:11.

Although, the backlash against the offering of thoughts and prayers in times of crisis is certainly well-earned when believers imagine that words take the place of action. God's people are above all servants. Our badge of identity, according to Jesus' prayer in John 17:23, is not our adherence to doctrine but our faithful and undivided love. Where we call on God to lead, we must be willing to follow. Into whatever battlefield or hospital room or back alley we ask God to venture, we must ourselves set to work.

Sometimes, though, we cannot even be bothered to legitimately pray for others. We can't be troubled to spend the time or spirit to name the suffering. We wave a hand and ask God "who knows all to do whatever is best" as if that constituted a petition. To intercede is to place ourselves, truly, deeply, bodily, in the place of another. To intercede we must first empathize. It is not uncommon for us to value others so little that we cannot be bothered to say their name aloud in God's court or to list their trials and plead for their relief, yet we rattle off our assurances to them that they are "in our prayers." To pray for someone is to carry them into God's chamber as if they themselves had not the strength to walk, to lay them at his throne and beg on their behalf.

Let us pray for one another and for ourselves with earnest and sincere hearts, fully convinced of God's power and his willingness to be moved on our part. Whatever we bring in faith will be answered with power. As Jesus hung between heaven and earth, between spirit and flesh, between death and life, so we too are suspended in this paradox of being. God calls on us to proclaim and to learn in silence, to plead and to accept, to demand and to submit. There is nothing flippant or off-hand about true intercessory prayer. We must be willing to be transformed if we are to approach God as supplicants to a mighty and tender-hearted king.

Notes for Chapter 7

Chapter Eight
⩵*Prayers of Repentance*⩵

CHANGING COURSE. As mortal creatures in a rapidly evolving world, our ability to change course is a defining characteristic, elemental to our physical, psychological, and spiritual survival. This doesn't always mean we were headed the wrong direction in the first place. Sometimes circumstances shift, priorities reposition, motivations change. At other times, we were absolutely headed toward destruction and only a radical modification can save us.

As a constant in our lives, our close conversations with God guide these processes. Prayer keeps us close to the mind of God and nurtures in us the wisdom to see our times and our choices for what they are. Transparency before our Father requires us first to be transparent with ourselves, to root out our secret self-indulgences and the lies we are prone to tell ourselves. In Colossians 1:9, we see Paul praying that the Christians in Colossae would be filled with wisdom, knowledge, and spiritual understanding. As we access these gifts, we are able to make thoughtful decisions and choose courses that tend toward the good rather than the selfish.

Even at our best, however, we still stumble, still look away from the Light from time to time and are distracted by the shadows. In I John 1:7–9, the writer says, "If we walk in the light, as he is in the light, we have fellowship with one another, and the blood of Jesus Christ his son cleanseth us from all sin. If we say we have no sin, we deceive ourselves, and the truth is not in us. If we confess our sins, he is faithful and just to forgive us our sins, and to cleanse us from all unrighteousness."

Two equally beautiful ideas are apparent in these words. First, that the blood of Christ continually cleanses us from sin. Our forgiveness was not a one-time grant given at the moment of baptism, yanked away every time we trip along the path. We live with our Brother in a state of grace that offers perfect peace. Secondly, we are made fellow-laborers in this condition. It is when we confess our sins that he faithfully and unhesitatingly pardons us from our guilt. We must acknowledge our reliance on him and our need for his mercy if we are remain in his fellowship.

Jesus relays a story in Matthew 18:21–35 which portrays both the untiring love and fierce justness of the Father. Peter asks him how often he should forgive his brother, and Jesus responds that he should forgive him seventy times seven, a metaphor indicating infinity. Initially this might seem to indicate that we too can anticipate God to be equally forgiving, but Jesus makes it clear there is a caveat. He tells of a servant who is forgiven a huge debt but who then goes out and attempts to extract without compassion every minor debt ever owed to himself. The servant's master, to whom he owed the original debt, learns of this and casts the servant into prison until he can pay every penny he owes—which given the amount, would be never.

So while God's mercy to us is potentially limitless, we can rob ourselves of that kindness through our own unmercifulness to others. If we are not willing to forgive, if there is any grudge we insist on carrying with us, then God will demand of us what we have demanded of others. The story Jesus tells seems so obvious and simple, yet so often we imagine our paltry prides and injuries more valuable to our hearts than the grace of God. When we refuse to forgive others, we are saying we count their offense against us as more powerful and more important than Jesus' sacrifice on the cross. The gates of Heaven are thrown open—it is only the chains we cast around our own feet that keep us from entering.

We might think that corporate prayers of repentance are impossible, given the intimate nature of sin and its remorse, but the failings of humankind are universal. We can all pray to be forgiven for our sins of the tongue, for our selfishness, for our greed, for our fearfulness, for our doubts, for our pride, for our blindness to the Spirit. It is good to come together and acknowledge our common sins, our common struggles, and our common weaknesses. Too often our time together is spent in pretense, trying to maintain the fiction of our strength even if we are drowning. Only when we stand in danger of losing everything, when our failure is already evident to all, do we come to each other and admit how bad things have gotten. If we live in the expectation that we all fall, that we all need each other's hands and shoulders and backs along this road, then when we reach that impassable river or lose our footing on the cliff, brothers and sisters already stand ready to catch us, to seize our hand and pull us clear.

In our private discourse with God, only complete humility and honesty are acceptable. We must acknowledge what we have done, and if possible, root out the true cause of our wrong. If I ask God to forgive me for yelling at my husband, perhaps the real poison in my heart is an unspoken resentment. If I had the chance to prepare a meal or buy groceries for a sick friend but didn't, was my sin simple selfishness or jealousy for the care others show him? If I speak ill of my spouse to a coworker, am I guilty of unresolved anger or of trying to lure my coworker into a closer, illicit relationship by winning their sympathy? Not only will this self-examination laid bare before God secure us his complete peace and healing, it will better equip us to resist evil in the future. A sin named and pulled out of its hiding place loses almost all its might.

In Psalm 32, the whole of which is a beautiful treatise on the power and majesty and tranquility which arise from the communion of the sinner with his God, the poet cautions that "while I kept silence, my bones waxed old through my roaring all the day long." Guilt is toxic. It eats at the soul and injures the body. While we are tormented by our secrets, we are unable to serve and love others as we ought. But as the poet closes out his song: "many sorrows shall be to the wicked, but he that trusteth in the Lord, mercy shall compass him about."

No sin, no selfishness, no dark and awful thought is too perverse for God's healing. We must not imagine that our wickedness is stronger than his goodness. Psalm 51 is another example of a person humbling themselves utterly before the Father. Even while admitting the wretchedness and ugliness of his sins, the poet is overwhelmed with joy and thankfulness. He has no doubt at all of the forgiveness of his God. He rests without fear in that love which is above all loves. "A broken and contrite heart," he says, "God will not despise."

Mercy, kindness, compassion: these are fundamental characteristics of God, and must likewise be fundamental to the characters of his followers. He does not watch us coldly from a distance. He is yearning, aching, for our company. Even when we abandon him entirely, we must only set our feet on the path of return and he will come running to meet us, arms open.

Spend some time this week openly, earnestly, unfolding your weaknesses in the presence of God. If you ask him for strength, he will not deny you. And like Job, pray for the sins of others. Be their bridge.

Notes for Chapter 8

Notes for Chapter 8

CHAPTER NINE

⇒*Prayers of Praise*⇐

IN THE WESTERN WORLD in general and in the United States in particular, we place an uncommon emphasis on production. We measure worth by work, stack up outcomes against outlays, and define our days by the imaginary red or black on the bottom line. As might be expected, this reliance on the concrete muddles our relationship with the divine.

At least with prayers of thanksgiving, there's a notion of tit-for-tat: well, God did give me something, so I owe him a bit of gratitude so I don't fall out of line for the next blessing. Praises, on the other hand, exist solely and entirely as their own end. For those of us who unconsciously or otherwise tend to run an account ledger of our spiritual life, time spent exclusively in praise is hard to justify. We don't walk out of that room with more stuff in our hands: we literally just went in, unraveled all those minutes or hours, and walked back out empty-handed. Wasted time, really. Think of all the other things we could have been doing, all we could have accomplished.

I doubt any of us would admit to thinking along these lines, but ask yourself when you last prayed only for the sake of praising and glorifying God, and you probably have to confess there's some truth to this. Perhaps it's never ever occurred to some of us to offer prayers simply composed of praise. But why? The Bible is full of them, throughout both the old and new testaments. Why wouldn't we feel an inclination to a tradition that's clearly innate to our system of belief?

Perhaps this has something to do with the fact that we're a western culture, and Christianity is an eastern religion. Early Christianity saw no conflict between the duties of the servant and the joys of the contemplative. For most Americans, the idea of a spiritual retreat is still largely regarded as hippie nonsense, unless it's safely relegated to a gender-specific weekend with clearly outlined goals and subject matter. In these cases, the activities are a retreat only in as much as the participants have retreated from their families in order to take part. They certainly haven't retreated into a place of silence and prayer and fasting toward God. If anything, they spend more time during that "retreat" listening to other people talk than they usually do. It's about downloading other people's knowledge and experience, not about listening to God. This may certainly serve a purpose, but it is not a retreat. It's a conference.

Jesus himself retreated often. He spent this time surrounded by nature, divorced from his reliance on society and convenience, in private dialogue between his own spirit and the spirit of God. He emerged from these periods strengthened and emboldened in his purpose. He did not justify to his disciples the amount of time spent away from them or list what he'd accomplished while he was gone. He simply left us this example: that to walk with God, we must spend time alone with God, and this communion is its own complete good.

When we praise God, we recognize in Him the impetus of creation and the sustaining of all that is good and true and pure and powerful in our world and every world. There is a strange and beautiful synchronicity in this acknowledgment: when we recognize all that is good in the God who created us, we must recognize all that is good or potentially good in ourselves. The Father did not sacrifice the Son for something worthless. The angels do not regard us because we are incapable of the lovely and the noble. When we find in ourselves some reflection of the image of God, we are able to find it in others. The more deep and pure and abiding our love for God, the more deep and pure and abiding our love for our fellow man. We learn to love as God loves: in hope, in possibility, in expectation.

A key element of praising God is finding him. When God is a distant king who has long since washed his hands of our mundane affairs, we can only approach him with difficulty and intention and time. When we see God in even the most fleeting and ephemeral aspects of his creation, we live in a state of constant praise. We glorify him in the fallen petals of the honeysuckle, the first tart sample of the blueberry, the hush of the dawn, the wild exhibitionism of the sunset. We hear his voice in the patter of the lizard's feet on the desert floor, in the laughter of the eagles, in the rush of rain over the roof. We recognize his gaze in the eyes of the homeless woman, our father-in-law, the policeman, and the person standing there in handcuffs. God's glory and power is as evident in the mosquito as in the elephant. And if we imagine that there is any place or any person in whom God's love is not present, we divide ourselves from him. We cannot separate others from the providence of God, but we can take ourselves out of his court.

The epistles of the New Testament are littered with constant and casual praises of the Father, Son, and Holy Spirit, as if the instinct toward glorification of the divine was ever-present on the lips of the writers. The opening and closing verses of nearly every letter are devoted to praise and convocation of the divine upon the faithful, and even throughout the texts, the writers frequently fall into a moment of praise. Flipping through the Psalms, a reader will come across song after song composed entirely of praise toward God. When we do not praise God, it can only be because we do not see God. He is ever-present with us and overflowing with good. The soul that sees him cannot help but praise him.

Although we have many examples of poetic and lyrical praise, we do not need to approach God with the language of flowers. I Samuel 16:7 reminds us in God's own voice that "man looketh on the outward appearance, but Jehovah looketh on the heart." God doesn't want our fancy phrases or college vocabulary prayers. He wants our open hearts, broken and blessed in their complete submission before him, perpetually awed and joyful in confession of his beauty. Training our eyes and our minds to see the face of God in all of his creation—not just the pretty parts, but the terrifying and daunting and challenging places , too—will bring us into a court of constant praise. The more we see God, the more we become like him, our spirits attuned to the real and the good in the midst of all that is dark.

Practice praise. Abandon the call to justify your time spent with tasks achieved. Retreat into true solitude with God and be at peace with his presence alone. Find the marks of his tools in even the most broken of vessels.

Notes for Chapter 9

CHAPTER TEN
⇒Transformation through Prayer⇐

TRANSFORMATION IS A MEDIOCRITY of the human experience. We are not only accustomed to it, we rely on it for survival. Our ability to adapt, adjust, even entirely remake ourselves to fit changing circumstances and necessities are a fundamental part of our nature.

Certain experiences we understand intuitively as crucibles. The death of a parent or the birth of a child are common triggers for metamorphosis. We cannot pass through these realities without some fundamental shifts in how we relate to the world and those around us. For better or for worse, these events forever alter who we are.

Prayer is such a crucible. If we walk in a state of continual, conscious holiness with God, the world itself becomes sacred. We breathe in expectation of beauty and grace; we recognize the hand of God in every molecule of creation. When this outlook becomes our automatic template, then we no longer enter and depart from the presence of God. We live in unbroken communion. Our mind is strengthened, hardened, disciplined to seek truth and eschew even the lies we tell ourselves. Our hearts are softened and opened to all the mysteries told by every aspect of the creation. Our souls are more able to find the divine in the flesh. Our bodies become traveling vessels and not mere jars.

But if we make a habit of inattentive prayer, we become dulled to even the most evident displays of providence in our daily lives. The person who is able to pop in and out of the presence of God without an overwhelming sense of God's power and majesty and love gradually makes himself incapable of perceiving that power and majesty and love anywhere. When we treat God like an accountant instead of like a king, we become nothing more than clerks ourselves, our lives relegated to a loop of mundane and pointless tasks.

In his first letter to Timothy, the apostle Paul speaks in 4:1–2 of the dangers of searing our consciences through hypocrisy. One of the easiest hypocrisies to fall prey to, without perhaps even realizing it, is the hypocrisy of prayer. If we pray without absolute confidence and faith in God's willingness and ability to grant our prayer, then we pray as hypocrites. If we call God Father and Creator but evince no reverence in our address, we pray as hypocrites. If we ask God to forgive us our sins as we forgive our debtors but can't admit to any actual wrongdoing, we pray as hypocrites. If we thank God for all that he supplies and then complain and bemoan our lack, we pray as hypocrites.

To walk with God has never been to walk perfectly. The Bible recounts many of Abraham's missteps and still calls him a friend of God. We know that David was the apple of God's eye and yet betrayed one of his closest friends in the worst possible ways. The apostle John, the beloved of Jesus, is also called a son of thunder whose efforts at self-aggrandizement are revealed without caveat. In John 15:15–16, Jesus is talking to his disciples hours before they will every one scatter and betray him, and still he says, "henceforth I call you not servants; for the servant knoweth not what his lord doeth: but I have called you friends; for all things that I have heard of my Father have I made known unto you."

In Luke 22:31–32, Jesus says to Simon Peter, "Simon, Simon, behold, Satan hath desired to have you, that he may sift you as wheat. But I have prayed for thee, that thy faith fail not: and when thou hast turned again, strengthen thy brethren."

God knows that we live in imperfection. He created us with all our weaknesses. The battle we fight is the one he has staged, and he does not expect that we will emerge unscathed, that we will never stumble on the field, that we will never lose our breath. What faith requires is humility and acceptance of our own inabilities and perfect confidence in His unfailing ability. Jesus doesn't tell Peter not to fall: he tells him that once he has picked himself up from that fall, he must strengthen his brothers, as only one who has fallen and risen can. Moreover, he tells Peter that the power to accomplish this comes from Jesus' own prayer for Peter. It is not only we who are transformed through our prayers. Those for whom we plead may also be wonderfully altered.

This said, it is better not to pray than to pray half-heartedly. If you find yourself hands clasped, head bowed, and thinking of pot roast, by all means, raise your head. Open your eyes. Don't offer God a false display of piety. If you're distracted, you're distracted. Be in that moment. Own your priorities. Maybe they are even the right priorities. If my baby is crying, if my friend is weeping, if my sister is angry, then the better part is service, not solitude.

If I am simply heedless, I should figure out why. Identify why I can't enter a place of prayer in that moment so that later, with intention and deliberation, I can gain entrance to that court. Prayer is not a *fake-it-till-you-make-it* proposition. If we cannot offer our God our whole heart in that moment, it is better to withdraw and rededicate ourselves later, when our mind and spirit are fully engaged with the divine.

Spend some time identifying what gatekeepers prevent you from reaching God. Sometimes it is nothing more complicated than a lack of confidence in another person who is ostensibly guiding the prayer. If we attempt to reach God through the words of a man who beats his wife or a woman consumed by heroin, it's unsurprising that we fall back. More useful is recognizing what obstructs us in our moments of private prayer. Naming and displacing these obstacles will allow us to approach God with a pure heart, devoid of hypocrisy and ripe for metamorphosis.

Chapter Eleven
⟹*Prayer, a Conversation*⟸

IT'S AN ACCEPTED RULE OF etiquette that the one who does the most talking should be the one with the most to say. In our brutish societies, we often define this as the wealthiest, most powerful, most fascinating person in the room. Sometimes our perception is a little less blunted, and we look to the person with the most experience or wisdom to guide the conversation. Rarely would we, say, allow a three-year-old to hold court for more than a few minutes of patronizing theatre.

When it comes to prayer, though, we often forget this principle. We regard our own voice as the only instrument of worth. Tunelessly we ramble on and on, as if prayer were monologue rather than dialogue, with God the Father our breathless and eager audience, waiting impatiently on the edge of his seat for our next demand, our next woe.

God defines himself as language itself. In John 1:1–4, the apostle writes, "In the beginning was the Word, and the Word was with God, and the Word was God. The same was in the beginning with God. All things were made by him; and without him was not any thing made that was made. In him was life; and the life was the light of men."

In our fallen state, language is fallen too: every tongue shaping the perceptions of the people who speak it by the limitations and parameters of that particular language. For every door that language opens, it likewise closes another. We cannot imagine what we cannot name. Every language we learn broadens our understanding of truth, and yet we find the summit toward which we climb farther away with every step.

As the Word, Jesus is not the embodiment of a language, he is the embodiment of every language, both earthly and divine. And that language is both the impetus of all creation and its sustaining. Language is powerful beyond our ken. The Prime Cause of all that is lies in the force of communication. The communion of understanding between one being and another. This is what God offers to us in the medium of prayer. When we reduce the gift he has given us to mere recitation, we divorce ourselves from the presence of our Father.

Instinctively we do know this is no small thing. Perhaps the reason we have repeatedly retreated from that presence by inserting false mediators in the persons of priests and saints and ancestors is precisely because we do recognize the enormity of an audience with God, and too aware of our own unworthiness, we fear to stand there. But it is our own Brother, that Word himself, who coaxes us into the room and stands between us and that throne. The conversation into which we are invited is ever warm, ever cordial. The laughter at our misplaced words and foolish requests is never cruel. And the part of God is not played with disingenuity or contempt. He engages with us only in the real and the earnest.

Don't let anyone convince you that God was laughing behind his hand as Abram begged for the people of Sodom and Gomorrah. Beware of those who argue that Hezekiah only persuaded God to grant the years he'd intended to offer all along. Some people will reduce God to the part of an immovable pillar, a deaf-eared idol who only pretends to regard the desires of men. They want you to believe that when Samson called out to God for one last gift of strength, he only fulfilled an immutable destiny. Prayer is a call that waits for a response, a question waiting for an answer.

And God is not always the one who will be persuaded. We know that Moses won mercy for the children of Israel through his intervention, but much later, when Samuel is enraged on God's behalf in I Samuel 8, God is the one urging calm. If we are going to encounter the Word, we must open our hearts to the power of that Word. Otherwise our prayers accomplish nothing more than the echo of our own voices falling back on us from the ceiling.

Throughout the old and new testaments, God perpetually represents himself as a being engaged in relationships. In the Old Testament, God relays tale after tale of his conversations and encounters with men and women and even children, with emperors and priests, with great fish and with donkeys. In the New Testament, Jesus primarily uses story and dialogue to reach the people. He speaks as friend and companion to people whom others in that society would not even recognize as worthy of the meagerest attention, to women and beggars and lepers and criminals. But he does not only speak: he listens. He allows them to ask questions and to challenge his statements. He acts out for his disciples the compassion and patience and fair-mindedness he expects of them.

When we pray, we come in a state of open communion with the Great Communicator. How sad it would be if the only voice we attend is our own. Faithful prayer begs belief in the certainty of a response. We must live our lives waiting on that response. God has poured his divine nature onto paper and given it into our hands. He has surrounded us with his continual breath of creation, sustaining us all and every cell, every molecule of the earth and sky and sea with his Word. Jesus assured us that he who seeks, finds; who knocks, is answered; who asks, will be given gifts. If we will believe anything at all, we must believe this.

So the question we must ask ourselves is simply this: are we listening?

Notes for Chapter 11

Chapter Twelve

≈ *The Perils of Prayer* ≈

C. S. Lewis wrote in his series *The Chronicles of Narnia,* in which Jesus is portrayed as the lion Aslan, that there is nothing safe about Aslan—he certainly is not a tame lion. Good and safe are not the same thing in the world of the divine. Throughout the Old Testament, God is repeatedly portrayed as a being mighty and terrifying, benevolent and unknowable, fierce and jealous, tender and entirely, impossibly Other. He is not a person to be approached heedlessly, nor is he a device to be used to accommodate a message driven toward a particular audience.

The Creator is not a trickster. He is not looking to take our requests, however misguided or foolish, and twist a blessing into a curse. We need not "be careful what you wish for" in the sense that God may choose to give us precisely what we ask for and then sit back and laugh as it undoes us. Jesus told us in clear terms that God desires to give us good gifts. When starving, we plead for candy, still he gives us bread. He is the Origin of all that is pure and beautiful and true and real.

In the New Testament, Jesus is most often angered by hypocrisy. He repeatedly condemns those for whom religion is a means of power and control and profit rather than a devotion toward God, an opportunity for abuse and manipulation of the less fortunate or less educated draped in the robes of a priest. It is a perilous thing to approach God as if one approached a stuffed animal or a stage prop. In Proverbs 28:9, Solomon says that "he who turns his ear away from hearing the law, even his prayer shall be an abomination."

Our God is not a pocket deity. We cannot ignore his precepts and pull him out when it's convenient. Isaiah 1:15 cautions that God will not hear prayers offered from people with bloody hands. I Peter chapter three goes further—not only does Peter state that God's face is shut against them who practice evil, he also asserts that God will not heed the prayers of men who fail to live with their wives in an understanding way, who fail to give them due honor.

It is not enough, then, to have a checklist of Christian duties all marked off and an empty sheet of sins. Our attitude, our love and respect and empathy toward others, has everything to do with the efficacy of our prayers. God doesn't say husbands shouldn't beat their wives if they want him to hear their prayers: he says they must live with their wives in understanding and while giving honor. Christianity is not a religion of absence but of presence. Our relationship with God is defined not by what sins we do not commit but by what good we do.

This is not to say at all that we must be perfect to approach God. At least, not perfect in the sense that we don't fail or sin or act selfishly. Our only perfection comes as God completes his work in us: we are made whole in Jesus Christ, not in our own deeds or words. Philippians 1:6 assures us that God who began a good work in us will continue to perfect it in us till the judgment. But our hearts must be sincerely, earnestly open to him and to our neighbor if we wish to approach his throne without condemnation. We cannot willfully mistreat others and then address him without shame or repentance.

Charlatans, abusers, and narcissists are far more at risk for such presumption than the average Christian (hopefully, the average Christian doesn't fall into those categories.) A more common danger among believers is that of the prayer as sermon or worship transition tool.

Any churchgoer knows what these are. Those prayers in which a speaker reiterates the high points of their lesson or recites precepts and teachings as if God needed to be tutored. Often the speaker will even slip up and use the wrong form of address, speaking of God as "Him" and clearly making him a third party rather than the object of worship. Sometimes the prayer is used as a vehicle for either scolding or encouraging the flock. Or perhaps it is merely a hastily muttered injunction with no real meaning or requests offered, just the direction to move from one aspect of the worship service to another.

Jesus spoke of other forms of prayer that are a danger to the petitioner: prayers like that of the Pharisee who offered his self-aggrandizing soliloquy alongside that of the humble and repentant tax collector, or prayers offered to increase one's own public standing. Likely many of us have heard prayers offered where the speaker thanks God that our nation is not like other nations, our church not like other churches, our leaders not subject to the foibles of other leaders. This is very dangerous ground.

The most perilous position of all, though, is the position of the person who does not even realize that they are in fact on their knees, prostrate before the throne of the Most High. It's somewhat confusing that our language uses the term "leading" prayer to describe the person praying on behalf of a body of other persons. There is nothing of the leader in the position of the petitioner. The person who prays is most servant of any, most humble, most venerate. If a person imagines that by kneeling before God, they have their foot on the neck of any other believer, they stand in grave danger. To be the person praying aloud in the presence of others is either to be like the Pharisees, with their hands raised on the street corners, proclaiming their personal positions as leaders of the faithful, or it is to be sanctified, holy, completely contrite before God. It cannot be both.

As prayer is communion with God, it is communion with one another. If in prayer we think that we achieve or hold status, we have missed the point entirely. True prayer is the opposite of power or authority: it is utter, abject, genuflection of the body and soul. If we insist on clinging to some shred of authority while addressing our Father, we have thoroughly misunderstood all that our Brother came to teach us.

Listen closely to prayers in public spaces. Who is being addressed? Is something being taught, or instead is something being offered? Are people chosen to make those addresses based on their position or based on their humility? And when we approach God alone, have we washed our hands? Do we bloody them on our brothers and sisters and neighbors and then call on him without remorse? When we say grace over a meal, is to silence and still the children, to call to order, or to frame a moment of quiet gratitude?

Jesus is not tame, and Jehovah is not safe. Prayer is perilous when undertaken by the proud. Beware.

Notes for Chapter 12

75

CHAPTER THIRTEEN

⇒Prayer: A Call to Action⇐

AND NOW WE COME to the point of it all. Spiritual pilgrims, we must necessarily end as we began: with questions. What have we become through prayer? Have we allowed God to work through us, and what is our work in this world? How does our continual communion with the presence of God cast light in the faint footsteps we leave on the earth?

We don't have to wonder whether we are truly on the path of righteousness or if we have wandered onto some other, easier, more comfortable route. Jehovah himself, in no uncertain terms, describes the prayer that he attends in Isaiah 58:3–12. He addresses first the offerings of the hypocrites, those who pretend at service but only seek their own position, before identifying what is truly acceptable before him.

"Is not this the kind of fasting I have chosen: to loose the chains of injustice, and untie the cords of the yoke, to set the oppressed free and break every yoke? Is it not to share your food with the hungry and to provide the poor wanderer with shelter—when you see the naked, to clothe them, and not to turn away from your own flesh and blood? Then your light will break forth like the dawn, and your healing will quickly appear; then your righteousness will go before you, and the glory of the Lord will be your rear guard. Then you will call, and the Lord will answer; you will cry for help, and he will say: Here am I. If you do away with the yoke of oppression, with the pointing finger and malicious talk, and if you spend yourselves in behalf of the hungry and satisfy the needs of the oppressed, then your light will rise in the darkness, and your night will become like the noonday."

This, God says, is true prayer. This is true fasting. Service toward those who can in no way repay us. Standing as the image of justice and love in a world bereft of both. No contemplation, no meditation on his word, can substitute for open hands and bent backs and weary feet.

Love toward God that does not powerfully urge us toward our fellow man is not love at all but self-righteousness. Flowery words and dutiful repetitions of what we know we ought to feel mean nothing beside how we do or do not serve.

Jesus promises us, "My sheep hear my voice, and I know them, and they follow me: And I will give unto them eternal life; and they shall never perish, neither shall any man pluck them out of my hand. My Father, which gave them me, is greater than all: and no man is able to pluck them out of my Father's hand" (John 10:27–29).

If Jesus is our shepherd, we must follow him to the heights, even of terror, to the valleys, even of despair. We must walk where he walks, among the poor and the broken, the grieving and the shattered. We must wash our brothers' and sisters' feet, we must count all strangers as our neighbors. We must welcome the refugee, feed the hungry, befriend the wicked, offer hope to the hopeless. We must pray and fast with our bodies and our minds and our hearts and our spirits, holding nothing back from God or from man.

Notes for Chapter 13

Acknowledgments

In addition to the Scriptures themselves,
the following works contributed to my study:

The North Face of God by Ken Gire

When the Heart Waits by Sue Monk Kidd

Help Thanks Wow by Anne Lamott

Confessions by Augustine

Holy the Firm by Annie Dillard

Thoughts in Solitude and No Man Is an Island by Thomas Merton

Discernment by Henry Nouwen

The Chronicles of Narnia by C.S. Lewis

The First Epistle of Clement to the Corinthians

The Epistles of Ignatius

The Epistle of Polycarp of Smyrna

Anonymous Epistle to Diognetus

The Epistle of Barnabas

The Didache